Daniela De Luca

It's a WILDLIFE, Buddy!
Harry
the Wolf

WORLD BOOK

World Book, Inc.
180 North LaSalle Street
Suite 900
Chicago, Illinois 60601
USA

For school and library sales, please phone
1-800-975-3250 (United States)
or 1-800-837-5365 (Canada).

www.worldbook.com

Library of Congress
Cataloging-in-Publication data
has been applied for.

Copyright © 2017 by Nextquisite Ltd, London
Publishers: Anne McRae, Marco Nardi
www.nextquisite.com

All illustrations by Daniela De Luca
Texts: Daniela De Luca, Anne McRae, Neil Morris
Editing: Anne McRae, Vicky Egan, Neil Morris
Graphic Design: Marco Nardi
Layout: Marco Nardi, Rebecca Milner

All rights reserved. No part of this book may be reproduced in any form without the prior written permission of the copyright owner.

This edition edited and revised by World Book, Inc.
by permission of Nextquisite Ltd.

ISBN: 978-0-7166-3519-2 (set), 978-0-7166-3522-2 (Harry the Wolf)

Printed and bound in China
1st printing March 2017

WHAT DO WOLVES EAT?
Wolves hunt such animals as elk, sheep, rabbits, beavers, mice, and birds. They also eat carrion (dead animals) and wild fruit, including berries.

ONE AFTERNOON, DEEP IN THE FOREST, Mother Wolf and her daughter Camilla are picking berries for dinner. Suddenly they hear a strange, crying sound coming from the bushes. Mom pulls back some branches and has a real surprise! There is a little wolf cub, all alone. "Hello," he sobs. "I'm Harry."

WHAT IS THE STORY OF THE WOLF AND ROMULUS AND REMUS?

A famous ancient Roman myth—a kind of story—tells of a woman who gave birth to twin sons. Their father was the Roman god Mars. An enemy of Mars ordered that the two boys be drowned in the River Tiber. The servant who was supposed to throw them into the river took pity on the boys and left them on the riverbank. A she-wolf found the boys. She took good care of the twins until a shepherd took them into his home. The boys grew up strong and clever. They built a town on the banks of the Tiber where they had been abandoned. This town grew into the great city of Rome.

Mom feels very sorry for the little fellow, and she takes him into her family on the spot. Meanwhile, Uncle Sven has found a dead skinny chicken that some humans threw out with the trash.

WHAT IS A WOLF PACK?
Wolves live together in groups called packs. The pack is usually made up of a central male and female pair, their cubs (often from several years), and other relatives.

Mom gently holds Harry in her arms as she makes her way back to her home in the forest with Camilla and Uncle Sven.

"The rest of our family lives just behind that big log," Mom tells Harry. "We'll be there soon. Then you can rest and eat. You must be very hungry."

THE REST OF THE WOLF PACK is busy preparing dinner. There is lots of work to do. A sausage is roasting over the fire, and everyone is hoping that Mother Wolf and Uncle Sven will bring back more food.

MOM IS SURE that all the others will welcome Harry into their family. They are always happy to share their food with others. And the wolf cubs are glad to have lots of friends to play with.

EARLY NEXT MORNING, the wolves are woken by a terrible rumbling and roaring near their home. When they go to look, they are horrified at what they see. The people have come again and are clearing the forest to make room for their farms. "What will we do now?" Harry cries. "Where will we live?"

WHERE IN THE WORLD DO WOLVES LIVE?
They live in forests in Europe, Asia, and North America. In the past they had plenty of room, but as people have spread farther and farther, they have much less space.

"What should we do, Mrs. Beaver?" Harry asks.

But Mrs. Beaver doesn't know.

"What should we do, Mr. Fox?" Harry asks. But Mr. Fox doesn't know either.

Even Rodney the Mole can't say what to do.

Finally, Harry asks George Boar, who tells him to go down to the swamp and speak to Simon the Heron. "He's a great traveler," says George.

HOW DO WE KNOW WHAT A WOLF FEELS?
Wolves express their feelings using their bodies.

Normal

Alert

Threatening

Dominant

Submissive

Relaxed or completely submissive

"Ah well," says Simon, shaking his head. "It's a funny old world, young lad. And it's not getting any bigger!"

But then Simon has an idea. "You could all come north with me," he says. "I'm just leaving, so gather up your things, and we'll be off."

IT IS EVENING by the time the wolves have gathered up all their belongings and piled them onto a cart. Simon the Heron flies overhead to show them the way, and the whole pack sets off on the long journey north. There they hope to find a new, peaceful home.

Harry is very excited as he marches along behind Dad, the leader of the pack.

As THE WOLVES travel slowly north, it gets colder and starts to snow. They gradually leave the towns and farmhouses behind. They meet very few other animals, but Sammy Squirrel notices the wolf pack passing by. He waves to them until they are out of sight.

SAMMY SQUIRREL

ARE THERE DIFFERENT KINDS OF WOLVES?

Scientists think there is only one species, or kind, of wolf, but there are many subspecies. They can vary greatly in size and in the color of their fur. Harry and his friends are gray wolves.

CAN WOLVES REALLY TRAVEL SO FAR?

Wolves can walk and run very well. They are strong and do not get tired quickly. Scientists tracked a wolf pack in Alaska which traveled 700 miles (1,130 km) over a period of six weeks.

Rasta Crow caws at the pack as it passes by. The wolves don't know it, but Rasta is watching over a mother bear and her newborn cub. They are safe and warm in their den beneath the winter snow.

Rasta Crow

ALL THE WALKING makes Harry very hungry.
He tries to catch a hedgehog but soon finds out
how prickly they are! Dad is more successful.
He manages to catch a deer by surprise.

DO WOLF PACKS REALLY HAVE LEADERS?

Yes. Usually the pack has a male and female pair, known as "alpha wolves," who lead. All the other wolves obey them.

HOW DO WOLVES HUNT?

Wolves often hunt alone, but when they want to bring down a large animal, such as a deer, they work together as a team. First they surround their **prey**, then they close in, leaving no way for their victim to escape.

Simon the Heron guides the wolves to a forest where they can make their home. Dad and Harry lead the way into a clearing, but just then a big male wolf appears among the trees.

WHY DO WOLVES HOWL AT THE MOON?
They howl to claim a piece of land as their territory. It tells other wolves to keep out.

WHAT CAN WE TELL ABOUT A WOLF FROM ITS FACE?
An angry wolf bares its teeth and snarls (left). When it gives way to another wolf, it lowers its ears and closes its mouth (right).

"WHAT ARE YOU DOING HERE?" the big wolf growls. "This is my forest! Get out at once!"

DOES EACH WOLF PACK HAVE ITS OWN TERRITORY?
Generally, yes. Each pack has a territory, or area, and this is where the members of the pack hunt for food. The boundaries of the territory may change in different seasons of the year. Outsiders are not welcome and may cause a fight. Sometimes there are lone wolves, who have tried and failed to start a pack of their own.

BUT DAD IS ALSO a big strong wolf. The two males start to struggle and fight.

HARRY JUMPS UP AND DOWN beside them, waving his arms and yelling at the big bad wolf. He helps Dad to win.

25

WHAT HAPPENS WHEN WOLVES FIGHT?

Wolves act a lot like dogs when they meet. First they look at each other.

Then they usually touch noses and sniff each other.

If they don't like what they smell, they begin to snarl.

Then they jump up and start to fight.

When one wolf wins, the other rolls over on its back and gives in to the winner.

AT LAST THE WOLVES have a safe new home. Mom and Aunt Flossie set up camp while Dad and Sven hunt for food. After a good meal, Mom tucks the cubs into bed. Harry is very happy but so tired that he falls fast asleep in Mom's arms.

WHEN THE CUBS are asleep, Mom and Dad look out over the valley. There is not a farmhouse in sight. "What a great place to raise the cubs," says Mother Wolf.

> ### WHEN ARE WOLF CUBS BORN?
> Cubs are usually born in late winter or early spring. At first they stay in a den and feed only on their mother's milk. After a few weeks they start to leave the den. They always go out with their mother or with another adult member of the pack to take care of them. Wolf cubs spend a lot of time sleeping and playing.

UNCLE SVEN IS HAPPY TOO, while Uncle Jack starts to howl—just to let all the other wolves know that this is their new home.

DID YOU KNOW?

Like all wolves, Harry is a wild member of the dog family. Some other wild dogs are foxes, dingoes, jackals, and coyotes, and they have spread to every part of the world. They are all quite similar in build, with strong legs and long, bushy tails. Domestic dogs—dogs that live and work with people—are also part of this family, and scientists believe that they are originally descended from wolves.

Glossary

Terms defined in this glossary are in type that **looks like this** (bold type) on their first appearance on any two facing pages (a spread).

alert - watchful; wide-awake

dominant - the most powerful; controlling or ruling others

prey - an animal that another animal hunts and eats as food

submissive - obedient; giving in to another

Note to the Grown-Ups: Each "It's a Wildlife, Buddy!" book combines a whimsical narrative and factual background information to help children learn a little life lesson and a few things about some animals with which we share the world. We have the animal characters say and do things that are not possible for them in the wild to create stories that can appeal to children and that they can relate to. The stories can help children think about making friends, growing up, and other important parts of their lives. The fanciful stories are balanced by basic facts about the animals' lives and behaviors in nature. This combination creates a satisfying and informing reading experience whether an adult is reading to a child or a child is reading on his or her own.